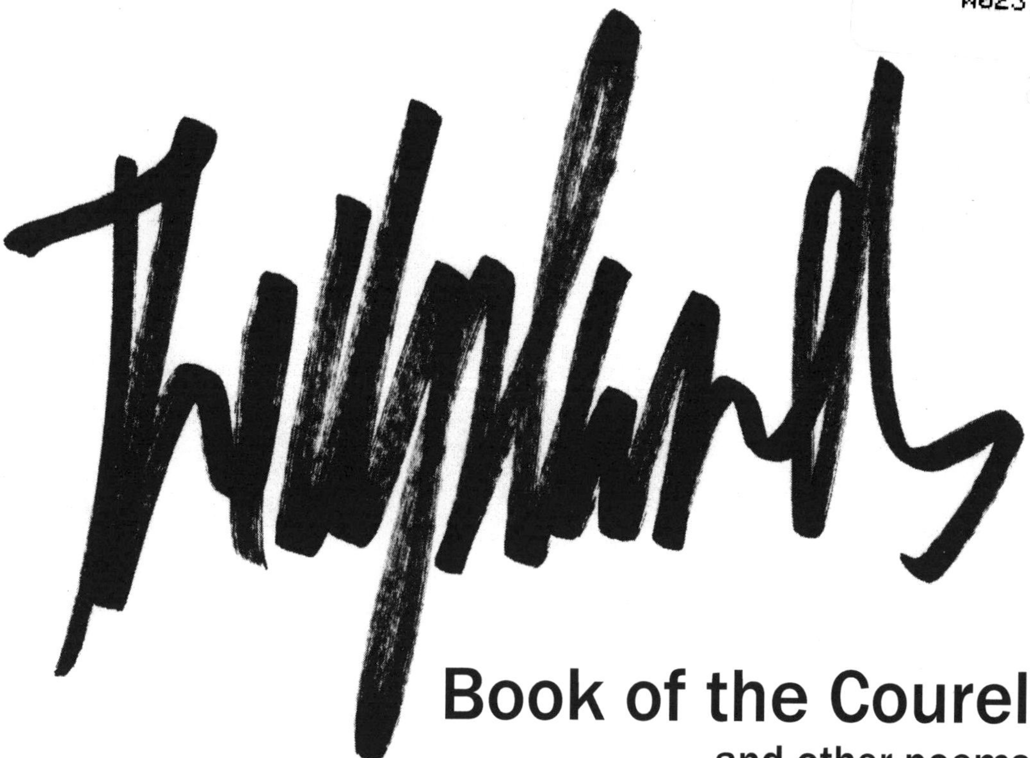

Book of the Courel
and other poems

by Uxío Novoneyra

translated by Erín Moure

with an Erín Moure poem from *Little Theatres*, a dictionary, an essay, an introduction, and dreams

VELIZ BOOKS

Interior page design: Erín Moure
(Moure considers the spatialization, presence or not of Galician, alternate versions, dissolution of text into the grey of Courelian fog or into faint pawmarks of wolves along the shores of the page, along with the greyed images of light, hills, and house, to be part of her translation of the poems for they help make the poems and movement of the work present to the reader, "as if they were walking in the Courel," she says.)

ISBN: 978-1-949776-04-1

This edition was published by Veliz Books with the collaboration of the Fundación Uxío Novoneyra, who provided the translator with a translation grant received for this book from the publishing/translation program of the *Dirección Xeral de Políticas Culturais da Consellería de Cultura e Turismo* of the Xunta de Galicia in 2019.

FOR BRAD

FROM THE GREEN HILLS OF MY HOME LAND, MY CELTIC LAND.

GALICIA

ALL THE BEST

LORENA

The Uplands:

Book of the Courel

and other poems

CONTENTS

UPTURNING HIGH SOILS

If you could merge the passion and seeking across borders of thought and poiesis in the American work of C.D. Wright, Cid Corman, and Gary Snyder, you'd have one possible avatar in English for Galician poet Uxío Novoneyra (1930 Parada do Courel—1999 Santiago de Compostela), for theirs too is work of the land. If you savoured the multitudinous dawn voice of UK-Norwegian-French poet Caroline Bergvall with the Shetland accents of Jen Hadfield and the attentionality to lexicon of Scottish poet Kathleen Jamie, you'd have another avatar for Uxío Novoneyra. There are echoes of Yannis Ritsos in English translation, too: a precision with things observed, an understanding of their simplicity faced with that of a human being, and a respect for those who work and endure with the Land.

So much poetry in English, that meets and greets us and creates its tumult and accent between us, also creates a space in us that is an avatar for this incredible poet, virtually unknown in the English-speaking world but a towering presence, even twenty years after his death, in Galicia in the northwest of the State of Spain. Novoneyra's a poet whose attention to his own culture and its influences on language and rhythm matches that which we receive in the works of the great Andalusian poet Federico García Lorca.

Yet we scarcely know you, Uxío!

Uxío Novoneyra—baptized Euxenio Novo Neira or, quite possibly, given the official restrictions on the Galician language that existed in his day, as Eugenio Nuevo Neyra—was a man of a remote and rural mountain past and of an accent shaped over thousands of years before it arrived in his chest and mouth and on his tongue. He was a poet utterly inhabited by the culture of his people, by its rich and nuanced knowledges, as popular cultures are when we delve into them deeply. He was a poet who gave himself totally to Galician particularity and who fought for it in poetry and in life.

Influenced by the medieval troubadours of Galicia and Portugal, and by poetries from Persia and China, to the Caribbean, through the Old Testament bumping up against the Beat Generation, Novoneyra was a poet devoted to language and to all that speaks outside of language, but which language yearns to attain or reach or bring to us. Having lived through the brutality of civil war, then the grey decades of Francoist centralism in Spain, then the wobble of a democracy built on silence and impunity, Novoneyra was a man who spoke always on behalf of freedom and the right of peoples to determine their destiny. He is a poet of the Land, of the equality of grasses and human being, of the weather, of the stones. Today we'd call him an eco-poet, for the ecology of earth was critical to him. He was not a poet who turned his land into nature or landscape or wilderness, but a poet of the steeps and pinnacles, of the deep ruts of cart paths, of air and silence, and the snow. He was a poet of silence, of the scythe, of water; his classic book *The Uplands* (1955, still in print and just as vital today) was one he wrote through as a life-work. It is not "rural poetry." It is the continual modernity of the earth. A poetry concise, tonal, rhythmic, gestural. And his calligrammatic poems are unique in any poetry culture.

In our day, when there is such anxiety of nations—for reasons both good and noxious— to assert themselves as separate (the US cancelling treaties with other countries, the peristaltic Brexit of the UK, the backlash against Catalan specificity and constitutional change in Spain, the unending pain of Palestine, and that of countries torn apart in Africa and the Middle East, the unsettlings in Venezuela, the aggressions of Russia, to mention a few), it is useful to listen to this poet who experiences popular savoir-faire and the avant-garde both as strengths, co-terminous in their possibilities for language and poetry and freedom. And who says we must listen to and heed the land that makes us.

As he wrote in 1957, as a man not yet thirty, who had to fight to breathe:

> ***Someday will I go from the Courel to Santiago across liberated lands?***
>
> ***It can't be that the force of our love is in vain!***

And that's *three* lines of poetry. The middle line holds *breathing*.

Erín Moure / December 2019
Montreal

Earth/Land

EARTH/LAND: "Mine is a poetry of the Land rather than of landscape, even though it has moments close to landscape poetry. Those who cohabit with the land never call it landscape." "Western culture had bred a huge gulf between us and the Land... an insensitivity. The Land was seen only as possibility for exploitation. There is nowhere that exploitation has not been envisaged. What's pathological about this is that we don't, instead, offer ourselves to the Land, allow ourselves to be enrapt by it." (*1997*)

"Arriving home from Lugo, where I was studying for university admission, I caught sight of the band of hills behind A Lomba, and upon seeing it, felt a kind of illumination, a levitation. It was an emotion that I never felt again and I remember it. I caught sight of a paradise. I was given an illumination from the Land. It utterly and entirely possessed me. I was still so young. It provoked a fascination in me, almost a levitation. The Land hit me with all its force. I felt a tremendous pull toward it." (*Telephone conversation with Emilio Araúxo, April 7, 1998*)

Wolf of the Uplands

Antón Lopo, ***tr. Erín Moure***

(A Story of Breathing)

In all of Uxío Novoneyra's extraordinary life, the years between 1952 and 1961 were probably the most enigmatic and intense. I'm not referring only to the fact that in that period, in the remote Galician mountains of the Courel, Novoneyra and the poet María Mariño were engaged in the "forgotten rites" of a "spell of moments," as she helped him find meaning in his desolation and he imparted her the gift of poetry. Nor do I refer to his times in Monforte [the nearest city to the south], with Roberto Martínez Andrade, venting the anxieties of his existence in late nights of wine and philosophical scepticism, alongside poet Manuel María, Novoneyra's close friend and contemporary, who was taken aback not a little by the force of the discussions and the inner fury released by alcohol. Nor do I refer to Novoneyra's pining after Clara Otero, a young Pontevedran he met in Madrid who later inspired several poems, nor to his exuberant trawling through the vibrant port bars of A Coruña in the company of Manuel María and Antón Avilés de Taramancos. 1952-1961, rather, mark a long period of respiratory illness, from which Novoneyra never fully recovered. In 1961, when the battle was officially won and he was able to return to Madrid, Novoneyra still took medication, notably the powerful corticosteroids which gradually altered his physical appearance.

He had been diagnosed with pleurisy in 1952 while performing his obligatory military service. At first he was sent to the Military Hospital in A Coruña, a stay that proved useful as it was near the Royal Galician Academy (RAG) and, when he had the energy, Novoneyra was able to go read in the library. There he befriended the librarian, Juan Naya, who showed him the institution's holdings. Years later, in 1987, Novoneyra returned the favour, offering friendly words of appeasement when writers occupied the RAG offices to demand the resignation of its president, Domingo García Sabell, who also was the official face of the Madrid government in Galicia and allied with Francisco Vázquez, the A Coruña mayor belligerently opposed to normalization of the Galician language following the death in 1976 of the dictator Francisco Franco.

Novoneyra's convalescence in A Coruña is worthy of note for another reason: it was there that the poet and his fellow soldier Manuel María attended the salons of Ramón Piñeiro,

Otero Pedrayo, and Carlos Maside, and encountered Galician cultural nationalism. These salons altered the way both men saw the world: Novoneyra learned to read Galician poetry differently, which changed his conception of it, just as his conception of all poetry was altered by his years at university in Madrid from 1948 to 1952. His long recuperation—from A Coruña he was moved to Lugo and, finally, sent to his childhood home in the Courel—gave him time to build a solid new poetic edifice from the stones of many different quarries.

Pleurisy is the inflammation of the membrane around the lungs, generally provoked by pneumonia. The lungs were his family's "dark shadow": his father José died of respiratory complications, and the cancer that killed Novoneyra was related. As a child, Uxío, his eldest son, was often near death from asthma attacks. Pleurisy, when acute, causes severe pain. Novoneyra's widow Elba Rei, and the widow of Manuel María, Saleta Goi, remember Novoneyra's illness well. Elba evoked, in particular, its long duration. She spoke of mornings in the 1970s, just after meeting him, when he'd come back from haying in the uplands nearly asphyxiated, barely able to breathe. He'd spend the rest of the day in bed, alone, isolated. We also have first-hand testimony in letters that Novoneyra wrote to Manuel María, published by the Centro Ramón Piñeiro in 2010.[1] In the letters, Novoneyra relates his discomfort and pain. "It's horrible, only comparable to the desolation of these lonely mountains. Just imagine... it's as if the weight of the entire sky were pressing down on me. It's the tragic side of the Courel, wherein the mountains invoke infinite loneliness and darkness." To which he added: "It's sad to think that we are all alone here and what lies ahead is death."

With his meticulous semantic and syntactic scalpel, Novoneyra's most harsh and effective poetic move in *The Uplands* is to make spaces recursive, whether that space be body, mountain, or river.

After a few months in the Courel, the buds of *The Uplands* started to open in the Courelian chestnut woods amid the noises and silences perceived by Novoneyra from his bed, or from the wide hall of his house, which he'd reach exhausted; it was the only walk that he could manage with

[1] *i en todo silencio preguntado. Celebración de Uxío Novoneyra II (1930-1999)*. Ed. Luís Cochón, Luís Alonso Girgado, Élida Abal Santórum, Alexandra Cillero Prieto. Cadernos Ramón Piñeiro XVI: 2010.

his damaged lungs. After a while, his ear began to perceive, in the Galician language of his parents, and in his own timbres, a whole inheritance of lived experience. He revised his Madrid poems to fit into the new structure he was evolving, and reworked more recent compositions, refining them, listening to them, and returning to refine them again.

The project was complex, relentless, and unforgiving. *Complex* because the songlike verses of the pamphlet *Snowflakes*, published by Follas Novas and edited by Girgado and Cochón, had given way to poems composed in a more hushed music, existentialist in their rhythms, which surely would never have existed without the Heidegger absorbed from Piñeiro and, above all, without the contemplative abyss Novoneyra had entered as a result of being ill. "The wolves of pain have gone now. In their midst, I really felt what longing is," he wrote to Manuel María in November of 1953.

Relentless, too, because Novoneyra was forever mulling lines, rewriting them, melding them until, at Galaxia, the publisher, his editor Piñeiro started to worry about mounting costs. Legend has it that Galaxia destroyed plates while the book was in press, so as to enter corrections, and *The Uplands* of 1955 was only finalized when Piñeiro put his foot down and told Novoneyra to stop. That's why Carlos Maside, upon first seeing the book, told the editors: "You fried this fish still squirming."

Unforgiving it was, because Novoneyra unflinchingly stripped every personal reference from the texts, any indication that linked the poem with identities outside the Courelian spiral, leaving poet and Courel face to face, alone, in an extreme sensory meeting, radical, body and earth coinciding in one shadow just as, at the roots of a chestnut, the tree coincides with its own humus. With his meticulous semantic and syntactic scalpel, Novoneyra's most harsh—and effective—poetic move in *The Uplands* is to make spaces recursive, whether that space be body, mountain, or river. The discovery of spatial porosity and of a species of continuum between subject and object, regardless of which is which, as evidenced in his attributive phrases, lets us better grasp the direction that his work next took: into the expressive prolongation of the ergograms, into the independence of orality from writing, and into a notion of poem as perpetual evolution.

In *The Uplands*, biography is elided and sites of rising waters emerge: Novoneyra's deluges, overflows, spring run-offs. Personal anecdotes evaporate, leaving the residue of spatial memory, the topos of place, in which Novoneyra encounters an experience not his that, yet, belongs to him.

The most revealing example of this occurs in one of the first poems, "Hei d'ir ó Pía Paxaro" [Gotta Go to Pía Paxaro]. In 1954, before *The Uplands* was published, a version of this poem appeared in the magazine *Cántico*, but there's another version, either earlier or later, entitled "Letanía dos tesos cumes" [Litany of the High Peaks], dedicated to Clara Otero. The structure of both versions emulates the *cantigas* of the troubadours, the basic fount of formal symbiosis for the poet, at a time when neo-troubadourism was a tool of the avant-garde, pragmatic in the face of pressure from the dictatorship [regarding expression of Galician culture]. In one version of the poem, the refrain is "thinking of you!" and in the other "with my love alone."

In the end, Novoneyra exceeded the troubadour-esque, though the model kept resonating right to his last book, *Wanderings and Detours*—in the extirpation of biographical traces but also in his linguistic ellipses and material dissolutions. In these, some detect a mystical attitude. Indeed, his work can suggest traces of mysticism, for it emerges from an emotional and physical abandonment, from an alienation that perturbs perception. To me, however, he is far from mystic or pantheist. The word that comes to my mind is *shaman*. Novoneyra can take on this role not only as poet but also because he came from the last generation of a rural aristocracy that once served as intermediary between the people and the administration, as witnessed by his family's political involvement. His grandfather Ulysses was murdered after a political meeting, and his uncle Manuel was hunted into hiding after the fascist coup d'état in 1936.

Novoneyra might have easily identified with the role of shaman, given that he was later drawn to the beat poets, who were well-known for psychotropic experimenting, automatic writing, oneiric auras, and subconscious solutions. But let's not go too far: Novoneyra's poetry does not explore any of those literary paths in depth, apart from automatism in "Vietnam Canto," which he wrote in one fell swoop in the margins of the first scrap of paper he could grab: a daily newspaper. His poetry, more accurately, is hyperconscious, and *hyper*consciousness acts as its own hallucination.

I imagine Novoneyra in 1952, when he wrote the poems that formed main nucleus of *The Uplands*, lying in bed and listening to the world's noise from a fierce distance. I imagine him thus, though no person now alive directly saw or knew the Novoneyra of those days of illness. It's disconcerting that even I, a good friend, never asked him about that period, so key for twentieth-century Galician poetry. I guess I was trying to be discreet: I don't know why it is so hard to ask personal questions when soon all questions will be impossible. It's curious that death gives us permission to immerse ourselves in the life adventures of someone who can't now reply or correct us. But we do it, and in so doing, we try to examine and assemble bits of a truth now irretrievably lost.

I imagine, then, Novoneyra "nailed to the bed," as he said, listening from a distance to the sounds of the world. I wish I could ask him now if that distance predated his illness or was born of it. The testimony we do have of his childhood—indirect, obviously—describes him as dreamy and roaming. Elba Rei spoke of a distance in him that was impenetrable even to her, "a last distance, necessary to be authentically himself. It was his redoubt, his wolf den," and that distance—which bred him, in Elba's words—heightened his intensity. It dawned on those of us who knew him that Novoneyra, ever grandiose in his generosity, sought to maintain a zone of privacy. Is this the distance from which *The Uplands* emerged?

I'd say there are two distances. One would be, in hermeneutic terms, ontic—*inherent* to Being—and the other ontological—what Being *does*, in *being*. This latter distance had its start in an ecstatic state, a revelation that came to Novoneyra during his illness and decisively affected *The Uplands*: not because the book emerged from infirmity but because it grew during the passage out of illness. At first, he was not conscious of his own transformation and felt lost, beaten. In February 1954, months before that version of "High Peaks" dedicated to Claro Otero, he confessed to Manuel María:

> I realize that the serenity and almost inhuman pride that let me write *The Uplands* is gone. Along with peace, I've lost my love for many things. The land no longer keeps me company and monotony presses in my soul like a stone. I often think that if I could emit in one big scream all that is drowning me, I'd be at peace, but it's not possible. Bit by bit, as time passes, I feel a terrifying blasphemy grow in me. Against who? Almost every night, I realize in frightening dreams how many demons live in us. The lysergic world of Hofmann is one I can relate to.

In these words, with his illness already in its third year, he admits to the unequivocal extinction of the fire that had driven him. Clearly, at that moment, Novoneyra didn't realize that the door to *The Uplands* was not yet shut. Carlos Maside knew it when he held the first copy of the book in 1955 and told the publisher: "You fried this fish still squirming." In 1954, Novoneyra still hadn't fully integrated the dark shadow of the wolf that grants him a remoteness, a distance stripped and tragic, a disquieting fusion of identities, detached from any landscape-poetry tendency. "At some point," as Novoneyra says in his later biopoetics, Of *Stubborn Dreams*, "you arrive at the stage of **extreme experience** that hones words to the brink that the poem demands."

For Carlos Maside and Ramón Piñeiro
Compostela men, late afternoon

the words of this book ring true in the high lonely uplands of the Courel. In them, so as not to mar things, I only speak their names or let them move in their usual and natural cadences. /N.

as verbas diste libro son verdade nas terras outas e sola do Courel. Nelas pra non mancar as cousas sólo as nombro ou déixoas ir dun movimento seu acostumbrado e natural. /N.

ONDE SÓ queda alguén pra aguantar dos nomes
poño eu a ampla fronda
a redroma dun castiñeiro
e sentada á súa sombra xunta a longa estirpe do último labrego.

Non coma as estirpes dos reis
ciscadas en múltiples pazos e alcázares
e países diversos
senón as estirpes campesiñas
xeraciós e xeraciós
xuntas á porta das casas pechadas
na escaleira de pedra
ou nas raigañas fóra dunha árbore coma esta.

Estirpes da gleba
amosados mortos que nin oxa o sol de Xullo
cando se erguían pra gadañar co orvallo!

Gadañarei outro ano
gadañarei en homenaxe
non por que a herba volva tenra e igual
e defender os prados gañados á bouza.

Gadañarei coma nas grandes rogadas do Vrao
tralos gadañeiros sucesivos
lambendo con brío os calcaños de diante.

Ir e vir da gadaña canta a ritmo binario
sobre un fondo de roxe ou río contino.

WHERE one person is still left to bear the names
I place the ample canopy
the rootforce of a chestnut
and seated in its shade together, the long lineage of the last land-labourer.

Unlike the lineage of kings
scattered in manors and palaces, *pazos* and *alcázars*
across Europe and Africa
Instead, the lineages of peasant labourers
generations and generations
gathered at the door of shut houses
on the staircase of stone
or in the rootspread of a tree like this.

Lineages of the glebe
appearing from the dead and even the July sun's unstartled
when they rose up to scythe in the dew!

I'll scythe too next year
I'll scythe in homage
and not so that the grasses grow back high and sweet
nor to defend the meadows won from scrub.

I'll scythe as we once did in the great work bees of summer
behind the rows of scythers
licking the heels in front of them with brio.

Back and forth the scythe sings its binary rhythm
above a backdrop of ongoing roar or river.

The Courel, Summer 1995

COUREL of high peaks that gaze from afar!
Here it truly hits you how a man's a paltry thing...

1952

COUREL dos tesos cumes que ollan de lonxe!
Eiquí síntese ben o pouco que é un home...

CONJURING THE COUREL

Gotta go to Pía Páxaro to Boca do Faro
lay me down in the Campa da Lucenza in the clear.
Gotta go to the Devesa da Rogueira and to Donís
to Rebolo to Pinza and to the Chao dos Carrís.
Gotta go to Lousada and to Pacios do Señor
to Santalla to Veiga de Forcas and on to Fonlor.
Gotta go to Cebreiro and pass through Liñares
climb up to Iribio to Cervantes and Ancares.
Gotta go to Cido and to Castro de Brío
descend and walk by the banks of the río.
Gotta go to Céramo cross the Faro and then
head down the mountain to Oencia and León.
Once out to Pena da Airexa and Vales I've been
I'll head alone to an upland where I cannot be seen.

Dark SUMMITS of eagles!
High mounts of sun and water!
Ranges!
Solitary earth in the sun and fog!

The sun drops
face-first like a father to the flowering fen...

From A Lomba
from the vales and dips of A Seara
from the Serra do Rebolo
and the Carreiro do Sono
comes José de Parada
toward Viana do Bolo and Val di Orras
climbing and descending the fells
in a dream of come ye gone.

Before and behind him the long ranges...

VAI polo monte o camiño
outeando como un louco
polos caborcos do val
i as poxas do taramouco.

Cruza solo a serra toda
sin levar outra compaña
que a gran presencia do ceo
sobre o silencio da braña.

Eu non sein pra onde vai
méntral'o quedo mirando.
Sólo sein que eilí se compre
o soño que estoun soñando...

TO the mountain heads the path
veering up like crazy
through the valley gorges
and the stepstones of the tor.

Alone it crosses all the ranges
with no other company
than the huge presence of the sky
above the silence of the fen.

I know not where it heads though I'm
gazing right at it.
I only know that there the dream
I'm dreaming comes to be...

DARK earth of the mountains!
Soil so rich that its entrails
both spill and store water!

Hardswept LANDS of the Freixeiro!
Mountain steeps!
Poor villages
who've endured in its bones!

TERRAS érmedas do Freixeiro!
Montes irados!
Pobos pobres
que se foron quedando nos ósos!

Roughswept LANDS of the Freixeiro!
Mountain steeps!
Hardscrabble villages
that endure in its bones!

Roughswept LANDS of the Freixeiro!
Mountain steeps!
Poorscrabble villages
left clenched in its bones!

Harshswept LANDS of the Freixeiro!
Mountain steeps!
Poor villages
hanging on by skin and bones!

The trail rises
drops twists
and fades afar...

JOSÉ of PARADA heads down
solo through
the Devesa do Rebolo.

Ambling he turns
his horse through vineyards
toward Viana do Bolo.

Leaving peaks in the past
his soul signed now
by the ache of the road.

O camiño sobe
baixa torce
e morre ó lonxe....

Vai o José de Parada
atravesando il solo
a Devesa do Rebolo.

Cabalgando vagariño
cruza a terra do viño
cara Viana do Bolo.

Deixa a serra pasada.
Leva a alma asiñada
ca mágoa do camiño.

HIGH AND clear lands at Lucenza
where the far ranges stare close!

Eagles soar with spread wings
lifting shadow across pale clefts
and grasses golden and bleeding.

I am what I see and what sees me:

. . . .

Cebreiro! Faro! Iribio! Cervantes!
Ancares!
Capeloso!
Montouto! Rebolo!
Dark pinnacles of the Courel!
Long ranges
of Oencia and Val di Orras!

The heart
trapped in the ancestral quell of the peaks
feels only the presence of sun...
Immensity of land and sky!

MOREDA full of mulberries!
Walnuts ashtrees of A Barxa!
The Boca do Couto! As Augas
and the Devesa da Rogueira!

Down through woodland
from the Fontiña da Rosa
to the mill in the ivy
the water chips at the stones
a bull nuzzles the gateways
young girls weave cloth
vapours fume from a far mountain
and the blond bull is bellowing...

WHITESPRINGS of the Rogueira!
Bush choked with heather and sweet broom!
Hazels yews beeches hollies and oaks!

Deepstruck timber!
Freshets for roe deer!
Darkmaw gulley-torrents!
There's no temple more vast
nor creed other
than this silence...

AUGAS Brancas da Rogueira!
Bouzas pechas d'uces e xestas!
Abrairas teixos faias xardois e reboleiras!

Outo bosco calado!
Fontiñas do corzo!
Carrozos picafondo!!
Non hai outro templo máis vasto
nin outro credo
que este silencio...

WINDOW of Lady Ildara
in the rockface of the tor!

Castelo do Carbedo perched
lorn on the clifftop in afternoon!

Lady Ildara of the Castillo do Carbedo was legendary. A medieval noblewoman, she interceded with the Condes on behalf of her people to protest the abuses to which they were subject, gave protection to pilgrims on their way to Santiago de Compostela, and was protector of the "Couto do Caurel," the wider area known as the Courel. Ildara left a mark on her culture that ran deep, and she is remembered today. Barely eighteen, she left the Courel after being given in marriage to Ruy Fernández de Melo. Her castle at Carbedo was granted in 1181 to the Order of Santiago by Nuño Peláez and his wife Alda. Some say that King Afonso II, O Casto (759 – 842), had once lived there as a child. This castle is today ruined and abandoned. Galicians also call high-fallen boulders and bare rockfaces "castelos" or castles... as if all castles were fallen, and all huge rocks were from castles, or as if the land itself were castle.

DEN of Lady Briosa!
Lakes springs heights
of Seara! Campo Lerín! Murelos!
Domain of deer!

Yes, there is a lot of exclamation in the poems of Novoneyra. As N has written, it is a form of love.

Dark dreams and strange snorts in the night
rough-hedged on the paths of the mountain.

The wolf

WOLF pits!
Gorges for wild boar!
Forlorn uplands
where no one's been or needs to go!

Wolf! Eyes and loin of wolf!

Deep in the eye of the forest, the wolf
moves amid shoots of yew
Snarling in the rut of trails
seeking hollows more scarce and more scary...

It stalks
Halts and bellows
Claws earth lifts muzzle and howls at the sky
With every shadow of night in its maw.

THE WOLF dwells in O Fedo
in A Lamelalonga in the fens
of O Noval o'r the glen
at the rockcrop in A Poxa
at A Lomba
in the uplands most distant and silent
where it's prey to nobody.

It snows in the Chao do Toxedo and
the Carboeiros.
The wolves stalk full-bellied through
steepfields of broomwood...

NORTHERN reach
of the snowbells!
Flowering smoke!

Ultimate NORTH
of the snowbells!
Flower of smoke!

NORTHERN limit
of the snowbells!
Smokepuff-blooms!

unravelled WHITE
blankets
of fog
howling through vales
through woods
and forest yellows
seeking out a hollow
or a high steep vale
to couch them
and let them rest!

Loose threads of fog
rising
and dropping
in the cage of air
across barren ranges
and through the stripped forests
of December!

WIND roams free across the uplands
with its wings full unfurled
roars in the chestnut woods
rips slates from the roofs
and jangles at the doors...

Anda o vento ceibe polos eidos
con tódalas áas soltas
empreña os castiñeiros
ripa as lousas dos teitos
i escachafoula nas portas...

SNOWBELLS bend low...
Their own souls held close
turned so deeply silent
they can neither do nor dare.

DOBRAN as campás da neve...
A alma de seu gardada tornouse
inda máis calada
e nin pode nin se astreve.

WATCH the cordmakers braiding new cord!
Field labours are done.
The snows came. Rain and wind awaits all
who can't tarry inside.

Me in mine
each in their own has
bread has firewood
hay for the oxen
and then
let come what may come:
It's the prayer
of the labourer.

Fatten up hogs butcher them
salt them and smoke them.
Keep rendering the fat...
Keep close to the embers...
Always something needs doing in the house.

IT'S THE time of roasted chestnuts
and settling close to the fire.
Through breath and smoke
          you see us clear.

1952

VEO o tempo dos bullós
e de porse tral'o lume.
Polo alento e polo fume
          has indilgar de nós.

NEVA no bico do cume
neva xa pola ladeira
neva no teito e na eira.

....
....
....

Eu a ollar pro lume
i o lume a ollarme.
O lume sin queimarme
fai de min fume...

IT SNOWS atop the peaks
snows now down the slope
snows on roof and yard.

....
....
....

I'm eyeing the fire
and the fire's eyeing me.
Without burning me, the smoke
makes me into smoke...

FALL snow fall fall
snowflake on snowflake
not even wind swirls it
nor does water melt it.

. . . .

Cido Castro de Brío snowed in!
Snow creeps right down to the meadows...

CAI a neve cai cai
falopiña a falopiña
nin o vento a arremuiña
nin a auga a desfai.

. . . .

Cido Castro de Brío nevados!
Baixa a neve ate os prados...

IT SNOWS blows and fumes.
Folks draw close in the room
to be warmed by the flame
till there remain only embers.

Outside on the roof tiles
through holes in the eaves
each flake floats awhile
then spins its weave...

NEVA venta e fai fume.
Vense a xente tralo lume
i axóugase toda encol
ó cariño do remol.

Fora riba do lousado
óllase por un furado
nevar a copo tendido
e logo a entretecido...

IT'S TIME we were off to bed.
The fire no longer gives smoke
or flame.
After all the tales told
there's nothing left
of the wish to speak.
The eye of the fire
joins all gazes in one...

....

The ashes of the bonfire lie
heaped in the hearth.

Besotted SPINNER
who spins aside the fire
her eyes fixed in the flicker
red white and blue.

Spinning girl who spins
nights of long winter
the finest filaments
from strands of thought.

Outside snow settles
upon rooftops deepstruck
while you spin and dream
of some far-off sweet thing...

—SPINNING girl so lissome
always aspinning
aspinning and dreaming
with nothing to show.
—With nothing to show
oh that's still to be seen
as with the fibres of linen
in twisting them lean
something's bound to get caught.
—Something's bound to get caught
and good faith you are right
for I've had my eye on you
not realizing quite—
I've been caught up with falling in love.

Dry FERNS of Winter! Fernery
of the Val Arcón and Fontela!
Doddered patches of time
scattered here and there all across the ranges!

FREEZE.
It's a cold that burns.
Bit by bit
the earth heaves up wetclods.
Freezeclumps snowbergs icicles!
A wolf stalks by...
Foliage rustles in the paths
deep down in the pit of the darkmaw.

NORTHFACE of the Val d'Asnela and Os Pradairos
down from Fonte Preta! The sun ducks
past there
howling across the crags...
Lands of ice from high December to Lent!
Snowbanks on the waysides and icicles on the roofs.
Shivery lands of Parada and Sant'Eufemia!
White and black ice!
Chestnut woods of the Estreito!
Meadows of the Veiga do Couso!
Nettles cow-parsnip ferngrass thistles and sorrel!

COWS graze
in the turnip rows.
The calf wobbles
at the'r side.
Feburary sleets
Feburary freezes
Feburary snows
snow so feathery...

PACEN as vacas
na nabarega.
Treme a pequena
que vai co'elas.
Frebeiro chove
frebeiro xea
frebeiro neva
neva lixeira...

YES THIS is what it means to rain and blow!
What a night for sailors and those tramping the road!

Curled up in my warm bed
blankets tight to my ears
I feel the capstones clatter
between the wind's whistling...

It CLAPPED blew and poured.
The land was kissed by sky.
Night's fall yesterday
could only be heard not seen.

The river brimmed. Springs rose
and mountain trickles roared.
Water swells into deluge.
Meadows soak in its cascade.

TRONOU ventou e choveo.
Bicouse a terra co ceo.
A noite que onte caíu
sólo foi para quen a oíu.

Ameteo o río. Ameteron as
fontes
i os fontegallos dos montes.
Naz'a auga a golforón.
Regan os prados a cachón.

It CLAPPED blew and poured.
Land now is sky's ford.
Day fast disappeared
into night, can you hear?

Brimming river. Springs risen,
mountain trickles roar, listen!
Newborn waters surge yet.
In their cascade, meadows drip, ~~dark~~ wet...

SPRING snowpack in the Fedo
and the Lamelalonga!

High peaks
of tree heath and ling heather
in buttery sun!

Wind HUMS and shimmers through high heather.
Sun winks and rises in the fog.
Through the mountains fall and rise
long shadows jagged and black...

/

The fogs glide above the fens
and on the mountain there's patches of sun.

Leaning over the weir
I'm transfixed in it.

The fogs glide under the water.

The Lubicieiras WELLSPRING
borne from twenty mouths
Roaring a thousand-fold!

FONTE das Lubicieiras
nacendo por vinte bocas
Ruxindo de mil maneiras!

MEADOWS of Fontela
what wee grasses cover you
more yellow
than the frailest of springtimes!

Drip drip
drips the wellspring
from steepslope
into blind scrub...

mountain freshets so tiny they drip into scrub without reaching the meadows...

SHINING water glows and gropes...
Cuckoo stockings —late snows— on heather slopes
and into the scrub of the topmost woods
along the barren peaks that stood.

/

The winds came down from Rodela.
The fairs came
where the lass goes glowing cinammon.

Girls girls girls they grew
lasses ladies straight-hewn flew
girls whirls with whom to whirl anew!
The fairs have come. The feastings.

Whitefirst DAISIES
primrose and bitter!
Burgrass in the gulleys!
Leaf rot in the drainage ditches!

Someone's alive
in this morning air.

Woodlarks
orioles thrushes blackbiirds!
Birds and nestlings over the rivers
in the woods and on the flats
and flocks and flocks
of starlings in the furrows.

NO bicarelo do bico do brelo
canta o paxariño.
No mesmiño
bicarelo do bico do brelo.

for Branca-Petra of the Courel

AT the lip of the tip of the bough
the birdling peeps.
Right at the very
lip of the tip of the bough.

GONE are the fogs
astride Lucenza.
Lit up are the stalks
in the Chao do Longo.
Glistening are the slates
of the Taro Branco.
Howling are the wolves
out in the Fócaros.
Squealing is the horned owl
in Val Arcón.
Screeching is the barn owl
in the Serulluda.
From far off you can hear
the roar of springs...

VAN as nebras
ó rás da Lucenza.
Alumean os chotos
no Chao do Longo.
Brillan os bargos
no Taro Branco.
Oulan os lobos
nos Fócaros.
Laia o apertador
no Val Arcón.
Aturula a curuxa
na Sereulluda.
Oise ó lonxe
o ruxir dans fontes...

WATER slips over the slate
and drops into the pool
                    drip by drip.

Wave by wave
            one wave after another
waits until the one in front dies down ...

MEADOWS of Chao da Ladal! Down goes
                                        the dozy
                                                water.

Staring into the river
I'm still off wandering who knows where...

GOING going gone
path of air in the air through the air
heading off to where no one's yet been...

....

AFTERNOON speaks in whispers
and the heart hears it...

THIS afternoon the air is my friend.
I sink and sink into it.
If the air has its way
I'll end up as no one.

"... that floatiness the air has, when the air makes itself present, in the subtlety of silence, of still afternoons when the temperature is amiable. Which is to say, when the air is your friend. The air is so... it's something really physical. The air moving over the air, warm air over masses of air... and it produces shifts of air. What's amazing is the sensation of floatiness it gives... To perceive it you need an ear that's so silent, as it's so vague and quiet, you have to really harken to it...". *Compostela, to Emilio Araúxo, June 23, 1992*

THIS air is engrossed
in something I can't see.
The birds the meadows
the uplands gone quiet...

ESTA o aire enfexo
n'algo que eu non vexo.
Os paxaros os prados
os eidos calados...

THIS air does delect
in what I can't detect.
Birds meadows fill
the uplands still...

WITH face pressed
to the pane of the window
I watch threads of water
against the shadows of crags.

In the threads of water
already unseen
the gaze rests again
absorbed in rain.

. . . .

Threads of water:
warp to the weft of dream-threads
I am dreaming.

XESTAS frorida da Sítima!
Virtas de xesta piornal!
Terra probe sequiza
de penedo i erba-chá!

FLOWERY Sítima broom!
Highfens of broom laburnum!
Barrens of dry
crags and bunchgrass!

RIVER-meadows!
Freshets busted out and streaming!

On this log
when I came as a child minding cows
I sat and braided belts of reed.

I am sure I have another translation of this somewhere

RIVER meadows!
Cascades that roar and trickle!

On this log
when as a child I came with the cattle
I sat braiding belts from reeds.

OX bellower
downswept horns
at the ready!

Ox uncut
bull-headed
on the rut!

BOI burdión
de corno broco
aliñon!

Boi marón
de boubo foco
outeón!

Mountain OUTSTEPS!
Holm oaks of Tarela spook-felted in the night!

Along the rim of the peak
                                        and lip of the hillside
your lopped branches pointing to kindling.

/

Bent HOLMOAKS at Cido
and they of the Veiga do Lago!

These holmoaks
whose wood makes handles
for the sickles that keep them pruned.

I GAZE at black sky in primal fear.
The bee veers back to the hive.
The swallow pulls up short in its flight.
Fogs flee thunder when it sounds its omen...

MEADOWS of Veiga do Xal
of Cido and the Reboleira
where you glimpse the Royal Road
and folk heading home from the fair!

I walked down the paths
singing or joying
stopping every now and then
to knock off the burrs.

Every afternoon I brought home
strings of strawberries
and blueberries I'd picked
and I ate every one on arrival.

SWEEP of the sweeping falcon
past Noval and Fontela!
Fens of the Val d'Asnela
and the Campo do Muiño!

PENEIRAR do peneiriño
polo Noval e Fontela!
Prados do Val d'Asnela
e do Campo do Muiño!

There's no FLAX
                    field as smooth!

No mole's nosed blindly through it
no cloudburst's laid it down.

QUÉ liño
            máis igoaliño!

Non veña o toupo fozalo
nin veña o torbón deitalo.

How Galician has rolling sounds and English has striking sounds.
To translate the roll with the strike.

OX bellowers
from o'r peaks!

High thick-necked
strong backed
bullheaded
pot-bellied and
gaunt-hipped!

OX brawling
scrappers!

/

BELLOWING oxen and the brayed song
bawls baleful
wallows deep and rasps high
fonda e cebra
all along the mountaintops and through the fog...

Chove
na casa da probe…

Down it pours
on the house of the poor…

RAIN swells across slopes and vineyards
Water bursts into rivulets
and where riverbanks are paying no mind
water dances up leaps over jigs its footwork...

The yaffle LAUGHS
pecks beak into oak
The jay lets out a trill
casts songs where it will
and takes aimless flight
seeking a'n'other limb
that's near 'bout as trim.

Cuckoo fills the valley with its song.

The cuckoo SINGS, quiets and sings
from chestnut groves all down the vale.
Time passes and says not a thing
and the cuckoo goes cuckoo again.

Canta o cucú cala e canta
dos castiñeiros do val.
Pasa o tempo e non di nada
e volta o cucú a cantar.

Su cherries GLEAM at Rubial.
Wind runs through hay ripe for scything.

Even the songless sings
the cicada sings in the hay
the hay sings in the scythe.

/

The washwoman FANS on the lip of the weir.
The water's still. Runs sparkles mirrors...

/

Shade CALLS.
Already no chirps can be heard
from the birdlings
so near me they're sleeping.

SHEPHERDESS whose life's spent
alone on the mountain!
Shepherdess how you spin and sing
legs gripping the distaff!
Shepherdess how you sing and spin
white wool of merino!
Shepherdess how you spin and sing
as afternoon wanes!
Shepherdess how you sing and spin
at the height of evening!

ILDARA of Romeor
spins and sings at O Sumedo
as dawn glints its rays.

Ildara of Romeor
goes quiet and looks past the heather
as dusk ends the day.

HERE at last, the fine days of Summer: celebrations and toil.
Here the harvest moon and the scythes in the leys
the reapers the stooks and pounding echo of flails.

VEO o tempo craro do Vrao: as festas i os traballos.
Veo a lúa das segas i a gadaña dos prados
os gavilleiros as medas i o troupelear dos mallos.

O Incio

Toward Monforte de Lemos
peaks rise like bread.
Toward O Incio like ships
fogs rise pale and slow.

Toward Monforte de Lemos
peaks rise like bread.
Toward O Incio like ships
fogs rise pale and slow.

Monforte

I SWING the scythe each summer
through a hundred thousand blooms
that if left unscythed
would ne'r have been born.

From the feast of John to that of James
steadily swaying forward
'tween the birdsong of dawn
and the river's roar...

St. John's Day is June 24, following Firenight, and the day of St. James, patron of Santiago, is July 25. Between them is haying season in the mountains of the Courel...

I'M IN COMPOSTELA AS SNOW COMES TO THE COUREL

Branca Uxío and Arturo
they'll be here in the Future
we'll be here in the Future
to ensure it succeeds the Past
and you Galicia endure
though your roofs collapse
and snow falls into your hearths.
Though roof tiles collapse
exposing the attics.
In the room where I was born
and even in the bed, there's snow.

Snow shuts down the valley
it snows in the Corzariza
it snows on the outcrops
it snows in the high oaks
and in every stand of trees
it snows in the deep wood and on every sapling.
Snows over rocks and across the holly
it snows in me right before my
. . . .
It falls oh powdery snow.
Cai a neve polvoriña.

from *From the Courel to Compostela 1956-1986*

all the
snows raze-
d all the
fogs shred-
ded all the
moons
in fury...

ALL THE snows razed
all the fogs shredded
spurious windblown
all the furious moons.

FEED on memory! Go to the Courel hear Earth speak
in the Devesa da Rogueira
sip the waters and inhale the scent of primeval forest
then go to the high pass at Lucenza where the silence roars.

THIS rockfungus so hoary and fragile
is the quiet silence of the rocks that seeps out in filaments
and dwells at their foot so they cannot sense it.

Slow rockfungus
out of weir-edge and riverbank!

Fits and starts of RAIN in the shadows
rain down below and high above.
The air of dream in dream
water drips in dribbles...

Night enters the uplands...
Afternoon goes without even a sigh
taking its leave in a way
I've never known before and won't forget.

Que é a coor do ucedo?

Van os tesos pro Inverno.

É a serra que ó ceo se enleva?
É o ceo que baixa?
É a nebra
ou a brétema da ollada?

Non sein qué garda a terra
qué garda a alma.
Eu ben sein que é certa a seguranza.
Eu non sein se é certa a seguranza.

Eilí onde o ollar vai e ven un xeito
hai algo certo.
Ben o soupo de niño o ollar pirmeiro.

E inda ha volver teimar a teima.
Por onde me veo esta certeza
Heina volver perder e volver éla.

What colour's the high heather?

The rugged peaks enter winter.

Is it the ranges that rise to the sky?
Is it sky that descends?
Is it fog
or mists in the gazing eye?

I know not what watches over land
nor what watches over souls.
I'm very sure it's right to feel sure.
I'm not sure it's right to feel sure.

Up there where the gaze knowingly moves
something's sure.
The first time the child saw it he surely knew.

Yet stubbornness stubbornly prevails.
Wherever I feel this surety
Again I must lose it to find it once more.

A LETANÍA DE GALICIA

GALICIA digo eu / un di — *GALICIA*
GALICIA decimos todos — *GALICIA*
astr´ os que calan din — *GALICIA*
e saben — *sabemos*

GALICIA da door chora — *á forza*
GALICIA da tristura triste — *á forza*
GALICIA do silencio calada — *á forza*
GALICIA da fame emigrante — *á forza*
GALICIA vendada cega — *á forza*
GALICIA tapeada xorda — *á forza*
GALICIA atrelada queda — *á forza*

libre pra servir — *libre pra servir*
libre pra non ser — *libre pra non ser*
libre pra morrer — *libre pra morrer*
libre pra fuxir — *libre pra fuxir*

GALICIA labrega — *GALICIA nosa*
GALICIA mariñeira — *GALICIA nosa*
GALICIA obreira — *GALICIA nosa*
GALICIA irmandiña
GALICIA viva inda

recóllote da TERRA — *estás mui fonda*
recóllote do PUEBLO. — *estás nil toda*
recóllote da HISTORIA — *estás borrosa*

LITANY FOR GALICIA

GALICIA I say they say   *GALICIA*
GALICIA we all say   *GALICIA*
until even the silent say   *GALICIA*
and they know   *we know*

GALICIA of aches   *forced to* weep
GALICIA of sadness   *forced to be* sad
GALICIA of silence   *forced to be* silent
GALICIA of hunger   *forced to* emigrate
GALICIA blindfolded   *forced to be* blind
GALICIA earplugged   *forced to be* deaf
GALIICA hobbled   *forced to hold* still

free to serve   *free to serve*
free to not be   *free to not be*
free to die   *free to die*
free to flee   *free to flee*

peasant GALICIA   *our GALICIA*
mariner GALICIA   *our GALICIA*
worker GALICIA   *our GALICIA*
brotherly GALICIA
GALICIA still living

gather the EARTH to you   *it's deeply yours*
gather the PEOPLE to you   *they're deeply yours*
gather HISTORY to you   *it's cloudy but yours*

recóllote i érgote no verbo enteiro
no verbo verdadeiro que fala o pueblo
recóllote prós novos que vein con forza
prós que inda non marcou a malla d'argolas
prós que saben que ti podes ser outra cousa
prós que saben que o home pode ser outra cousa

sabemos que ti podes ser outra cousa
sabemos que o home pode ser outra cousa

gather strength and arise in the fullness of our language
in the living voice that is the speech of our people
gather strength for the young who arrive in great number
strength for those not yet marked by the clasp of chains
for those who know GALICIA can be something greater
for those who know humanity can be something more

it's we who know GALICIA can be something greater
together we know humanity can be something more

VIETNAM CANTO

PEAKS PEAKS PEAKS LIKE THESE PEAKS RISE
ONE BY ONE FOR EACH OF THE DEAD
VIETNAMMMMMMMMMM
VIETNAMMMMMMVIETNAMMMMMMMMMM
VIETNAMMMMMMMMMM
they put words in the house in the kitchen on the table .... in the bed already
and shut up shutuuuuuuuuuuuuuuuupppp
right to the cry that accuses you USAUSAUSAUSAUSAUSA
one
dead
two dead
three / thirty dead
three hundred / three thousand dead
TEIT OFFENSIVE 22000 / 100000 dead
all those returned as zeros oooooooooooooooooooo
underneath each of them 10 / 100 / 1000 / 10000 dead by the machine
the defunct that night hosts amidst reeds and under the thunder
of the monsoon
in the moonlight of TEIT

it's shameful to live
it's shameful to be alive and see SPRING

when is a people vanquished?
a people is always being born

is never done nevernevernevernevernevernevernever

this I know because of you
like my own people

GALICIA so small
the one and only

the dead the dead
the dead the dead
the dead the dead
the dead the dead
the dead the dead
the dead the dead
the dead the dead
the dead the dead
the dead the dead
the dead the dead
the dead the dead
the dead the dead
the dead the dead
the dead falling via teletype
moons of LI PO melted till their light signals the E of
FREEEEEEEEEEEEEEEDOM!

oh how much I have of you small as I am of this peace dead

undefined

nightnight
n / i / g / h / t smashed to bits
so that each bit holds only one man
standing
up

they enter the cities from the SOUTH EAST far away
yet really all come from the next village over
HUE SAIGON DANANG
with my own brothers and family
Galicians every single day
but they didn't forget it like we've forgotten it
so much nearby that at times they shout man
and
we look around to see who they call.
it's not me too

who's staying here
whom I'm killing there
luxating GALICIA as they luxate
KANSAS NEW JERSEY CALIFORNIA COLORADO
IOWA
such clean names?

pardon for this peace
PEACE on billboards beside COCACOLA
PEACEPEACEPEACEPEACEPEACEPEACEPEACEPEACE
plastered across an expanse of
wall

they'll hollow out the names
even so
the people are still there
I can forcefully say
your name can still be spoken among those who fell there
we can speak it
from then we have a name anew:

human people
/ MARÍA MARIÑO our dynamiter of LANGUAGE /
human-people
human-people
who were for centuries a people like mine
for years mine were a people just as they are

BROTHERHOOD GALICIA VIETCONG

between my mother ANA we love them
between them love ANA you
three students in LUGO without names
in VIGO MÉNDEZ FERRÍN   with him
and you MARÍA MARIÑO   CHÉ tears 1967

no
I know that singing out is not the same
Forgive me for spending time on words
which though sincere are much slower than the rims
and suspensions inscribed with the barrel of a gun

BALLAD OF MANOEL DE RIBADAIRA

for Federico García

Over the vastness of the ranges men climbing
at night came for MANOEL CELA called
MANOEL DE RIBADAIRA by those nearby

they tore his parents from his embrace
and it's said that it's said they brought him down
on his horse along the ROYAL road
it's said he promised them a twin-barrelled shotgun
and the newborn pup he'd been training
and as he couldn't use it in the future anyway
they could chop off a finger and take it
as proof for those who'd given orders to kill him

they skirted SAVANE and MEIRAOS
few saw them pass for all turned their gaze
and on reaching TEIXEIRA they went even higher
beside the deep pit they stopped and dismounted
he spun in the air when the first shot resounded
there then rang a second a third and a fourth
they threw him in the grotto without coup de grace
rained pebbles and boulders over his body
the shepherds of livestock saw and heard something
and the one with the sack brought back word

it was the people of PARADA who went and got him
they had to knot two ropes together

with them tied to his belt his father went down
lashed him tight with buckles and cord
they pulled MANOEL's body up after his father
brought him on foot across the razed mountain
passing through hamlets frozen by fear
marking steps as they bore
what went up alive back down on a stretcher
past the church cemetery on to SAVANE

back to the ROYAL road and up the people silent
all with the same hush weighed upon them
to PARADA they came where they were awaited
in front of the house all stood in a circle
there I saw it happen as a child of six
his sisters and mother raised a howl of anguish
until they collapsed one after another

it's said they were four who grabbed and killed him
and they died all of them in violent anger
they were four and their names I won't utter
even though forty years have gone by.

PARADA, SAVANE, MEIRAOS, TEIXEIRA lie in the mountainous Courel. The ROYAL road, a path between PARADA and SAVANE, follows the old King's Highway, the first public road built for use by all. MANUEL DE RIBADAIRA is MANUEL CELA MACÍA, from Parada, a musician at local celebrations and dances, he was murdered by the Falange on 16 October 1936 aged 21. His wrong? After a meeting of Acción Repúblicana at election time the previous spring, he had helped bring a wounded man to hospital, where he was seen by Rightists. The four Falangists who killed him were later sent to the Front in the Nationalist army (after protests by neighbours at their murdering and sacking in the area) and killed; one was killed on reporting for duty by his own commander, who was from the Courel and had heard of what went on.

CUMES mouros das aigas!
Montes do sol e a auga!
Serras! Terras solas ó sol e as nebras!

O sol baixade
cara como un pai á flor da braña...

Pola Lomba
polas vagoadas e os cousos da Seara
pola Serra do Rebolo
e o Carreiro do Sono
vai o José de Parada

cara Viana do Bolo e Val di Orras
subindo e baixando as costas
nun soño de idas e voltas.

Diante e tras del a serra longa...

Dark PEAKS of eagles!
Mountains of sun and water!
Ranges! Lands stark in the sun and fogs!

The sun lowers its
face like a father over fen-flowers...

Over A Lomba
along gorgetracks and darkmaws at A Seara
through the Serra do Rebolo
and the Carreiro do Sono
goes José of Parada

toward Viana do Bolo and Val di Orras
up and down steeps
in a dream of comings and goings.

Before and behind him the long range....

NEVA como eu poño
naquil poema neva.

NEVA no bico do cume
neva xa pola ladeira
neva no teito e na eira.

NEVA pecho na valiña
neva na Corzariza
neva na tara fraguiza
neva nos outos carballos
i en tódolos arburallos
neva nos soutos i en
todíñolos gallos
neva pra pena e pra aciña
....
....
....
Cai a neve polvoriña.

IT SNOWS just like I put
it snows into this poem.

IT SNOWS at the top of the peak
snows down the slopes already
snows on roof and yard.

SNOWS to blot out the col
snows in the Corzariza
snows on the outcrops
snows in the high oaks
and in every stand of trees
it snows in the deep wood and
on every sapling
snows over rockcrop and holly
....
....
....
It falls oh powdery snow.

TROUT of the River Lor!
Honey sweet and bitter to taste
Sheep and goat!
Eggs on fried bread!
Ash-cured chorizos in twists of parchment!
Cured ham
ember-toasted or boiled whole
in the pot!
The hoof sticking out
sticking out its hoof.
Fresh roe-deer or curd cheese!
Shredded pork rib cutlets blood crêpes!

Our own grey
wheat
and liqueur of blueberries
that still have their stems!

Chestnuts dry or boiled
or roasted or in milk
and a good
quiroga bierzo or valdeorres wine from renowned cellars
that as well as lifting spirits keep rites and rest kindled!

VOLTA a labrandeira a petar no cristal.
Sempre á misma hora chama en tódalas ventanas
xira encol da casa e volta á chamada...

Fai meses morreu miña mai.

It's the washerwoman come tapping at the pane.
She always calls at this hour at every window
goes around the house and comes to tap again...

It's been months since my mother died.

1973

NEW NAMES FOR PAIN

Night CLOSES IN over the heather
and I've not yet seen the heart of my girl.
Now's time to tremble and be afeard.

/

THIS disquiet! This thing! This deaf hand that pulls.
Urge to leave without knowing where to go!

/

My heart NOW is a festered sore.
A paw of the she-wolf moves to tear at the wound.

/

THIS audible pain!
This heart-mine!
This pain
This pain that I see for what it is
without knowing how it came to be!

/

It came like falling into a pit.
Once there was night and day
Now all is wolf blackness.

There's no you
and no house
no land
no arriving
arrived.

There's no heart.
Lie then
with the night.

NON estás
e nin casa
nin país
nin chegar
é chegada.

Cor non está.
Ponte
xunto á noite.

/

/

DIG the den deep.
Grief, enough!
Grief, leave!
My soul's done for.

CAVAR en cova.
Door abonda!
Door deixa!
Son alma feita.

1962

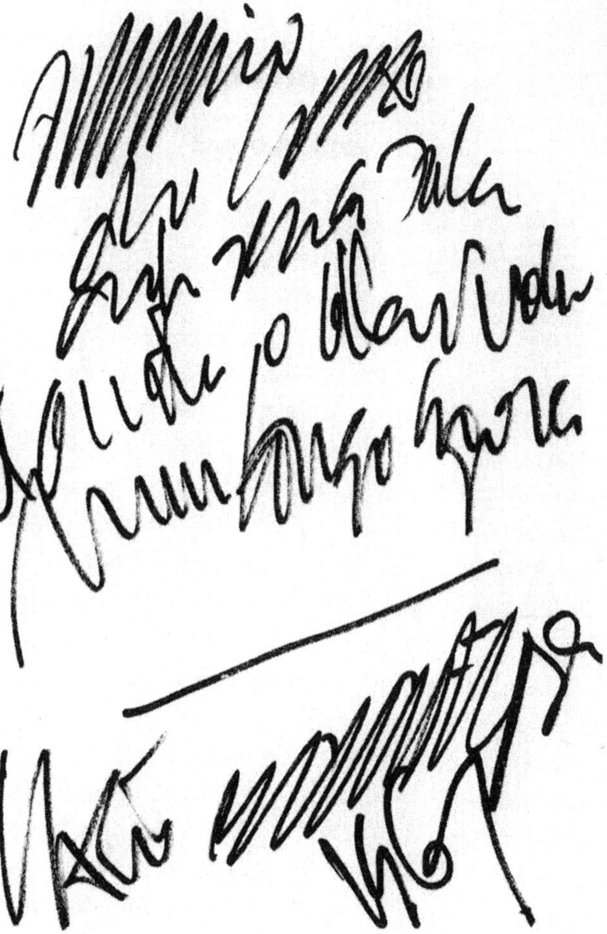

Submerged
in distance
Ah solitary range
that returns the gaze
in a long now!

Uxío Novoneyra
1967

Sumio
de lonxe
Ouh serra sola
de onde o ollar volve
nun longo agora!

Uxío Novoneyra
1967

*On Calligraphy:

...I have to create contrasting spaces, so that it's not all one solid mass.
Compostela, June 23, 1992

Even if language is infinite, the word is so saturated and left obsolete that it seeks an exit in a calligraphic marking. It's almost biological. A overpowering impulse. It precedes thinking, as the mark moves more quickly than the brain. That seeking. Pressure in the hand not yet in the brain. There's a process of warming up, as in dance: once you've done twenty, the real poems start to emerge... In calligraphy, the word emerges from who knows what force; it doesn't come from memory, who knows where it comes from. The crucial moment has remained inexpressible.
by telephone, November 10, 1998

*from the notes of Emilio Araúxo, in "As cores do ucedo" [The Colours of Heather], in *Os Eidos*, Biblioteca de Mesopatamia edition. Santiago: Chan da Pólvora, 2018, 268.

Elegies and Compilations

IN THE DARK OF MY ROOM

The book shut and a thread of sun
diagonal at this moment.

Leaves FALL.
In me I feel some thing
come to rest without even touching...

Non sei o que é.
Só sei que é e que non me é alleo.
Ven com'a chuvia no preludio escuro,
abre por dentro a sua estanza e faime todo remoto.

/

QUE tiño ó lonxe?
Vento do inverno, de qué che son coñecido?
Pura, eterna pregunta, ti sabes.

I know not what is.
I know but that it is and that to me it is no stranger.
It comes like rain into the dark doorway,
opens its space inside and makes all remote to me.

/

WHAT destiny in the distance?
Wind of winter, how is it I'm known to you?
Pure eternal question, you know.

—A Rosalía—

SOLA da Terra ti sabes que o ceo non é noso.
Poden inseguranza e desamparo i acolleste ós bés certos:

a casa! o val! a patria homilde!
Nosa patria pola que ti clameas furando a noite!

—To Rosalía—

ALONE on the Land you know the sky's not ours.
Insecurity and abandon may be but you cling to what's sure:

house! valley! humble homeland!
Our homeland for which you clamour in the pit of night!

1958

Elexía a Albert Camus

Estou velándote, exposto á noite...
Anceio é nova?

        Dun laio autro da curuxa
a pregunta faise contestada e tórnase pregunta.

Velarei deica que volva a folla.

1960

Elegy for Albert Camus *—died January 4, 1960*

I sit vigil for you, exposed to the night.
Fierceness is news?

        From one wail of the owl to the next
my question is answered and becomes question again.

I'll sit vigil until the leaves return.

SALGUEIRO da tara irada
xa non son aquela ollada.

A ollada vai
mais non leva nin trae.

WILLOW in steepcrag
Your gaze is not really mine.

Your gaze faces outward
but bears naught, nor does it bring.

LAST AFFLICTION

I ACHE to think the rain's not mine
and that the wind
and dark wideswept hues of the Courel
are not a thing left behind
in the ongoing loss of all that was created
to fall into the dull coursing
that will not last forever either,
so I know this ache means something
and is not held without reason.

. . . .

Oh affliction,
you never lead me to indifference!
In opening wider, the final void
clamours for creation.

UN, O Courel, January 1959
EM, Montreal, January 2019

ANGURIA ÚLTIMA

DOIME pensar que a choiva non é miña
e que o vento
i a coor escura e longa do Caurel
non vein de esta cousa que deixa
o ir perdendo todo o que ún creou
e cair no curso xordo
que tampouco ha seguir sempre,
pois eu sei que ista dor é por algo
que ún non tiña sin fundamento.

....

Ouh anguria,
ti nunca me levache a indiferencia!
O abrirse mais, o valeiro último
crama a creación.

"There's still some dream held in common that pulls us. Our poetic fraternity is, for the most part, rooted in the Galician language. Still, when I think of fraternity, I think of those who worked on the land. Even though I didn't work with them everyday, I still think of them when I think of fraternity. Clearly, we coincide in one fraternal image because all of us are created and sustained by the Language. The Language is a living image, a continual and very intense image of all that is the past. For me, single images matter less than this continual image. Our Galician past is rural and working class, and our fraternity still has power, even if it seems that what I'm describing is out of tune with the present. Emotions aren't fads and we can't choose what makes us feel fraternity. History chooses for us."

A COURELIAN VOCABULARY (from these poems and others)

+ only in English; * in Galician and English; √ in a poem not in this book

Abeseda	northface, mountainside that faces north, northscarp +
Aira	treadflats, threshing floor, treading ground √
Beirón (da presa)	lip (of a weir) +
Bico (do cume)	crest, top, tip, highest point of mountain summit *
Bosque	forest, a more general word than *devesa, fraga, souto* +
Bouza	scrub, brush, bush; land not forest but uncultivated *
Braña	fen (river-washed humid or wet meadow with grass good for grazing) *
Caborco	gorge, dizzyingly steep and narrow gulley *
Calzas do cucu	late spring snowfalls, literally "cuckoo stockings" (fallen after the return of the cuckoos—a sign of spring) +
Campa, campaza	haymoll, flatter stretch of grasses between slopes (where erosion from higher up has made soil rich and grasses naturally plentiful)*
Carambelo (pedra)	icicle (dripstone, stalactite) + (√)
Carrozo	steep and deep gulleyed torrent *
Cemba	embankment, mound +
Comba	glen +
Cortiña	kitchen garden, fenced vegetable/fruit garden by the house
Couso	darkmaw, hole in the ground used for wolf-trap *
Cume	peak, high summit *
Devesa	primeval mixed forest (Atlantic and Mediterrean flora) of tall trees that grow on north slopes away from sun *
Eido	upland, steepslope dear to its cultivator, sown for thousands of years. "Language already knows what the land is." *

Fraga	mixed Atlantic forest, seems wild but many trees were once planted by humans √
Ladeira	mountainside slope, flank *
Nabarega	turnip patch (prized for its greens); season when cattle are let into the turnips to graze (the turnips are fed to pigs later on)
Pena	high rockcrop emerging naturally from more gradual land, jutting, steepjut *
Penedo	crag, ragged tor emerging from a high slope or steep *
Pestanas (da pena)	rockcrop overhangs √
Picafondo	deepsharps, "touchbottoms", darkmaw *
Pincheiras	pinchfalls, creeks or rivers falling in multiple waterfalls over penas and outcrops √
Poxa	outstep, rock that sticks out of a rock wall that you can use to climb the wall; staggers; stepstones: projecting stones *
Prado	meadow, ley, sward *
Prado do río	fen, rivermeadow √
Raigaña	rootspread, conjunction of spreading roots, energy of roots to keep growing despite being cut or damaged or killed *
Redroma	rootforce, thicket of shoots or suckers that grow up from the roots of a tree *
Reprexos	manmade earthdams in sloped *soutos* to support the tree roots; √
Restrellas	mountain ryefields, rye uplands √
Serra	range (horizon of mountains), cordillera, chain *
Souto	groves of planted chestnuts, up to 800 years old, whose wide limbs touch in the sky and hold humidity in the ground they shade; a climate in itself created by the trees for the trees *
Tara	flat outcrops, tors, smooth peakrock on which no trees or grass grow *

Tara irada	steepcrag, rampart *
Taramouco	outcrop, tor, cragknot that stands out on a rockface, spur *
Teso	high peak, rugged peak "not all the cumes are tesos" *
Trempo	wetclod, a clump of half-frozen earth, icy on the bottom +
Trouso	snowberg, snowbank still left in spring in the shady steeps +
Tourón	freezeclump, frozen clump of earth or sod +
Uces (uz)	tree heath, heather +
Ucedo	high heather field, thornthicks *
Vagoada	gorgetrack, narrow pass and trail between mountains *
Valiña	col, small narrow creek valley *
Veiga	rich bottomland along a river, cultivated *
Virta (seara)	highfen, often sown in wheat or rye, at times back to bouza *
Xesta	broom, sweet broom, its branches used for roof thatch, *and for the raincoats pictured by Ruth Matilda Anderson in the 1930s in Pontevedra, for example...* *
Xestedo:	broomwood +

Courelians traditionally walked in the steeps and the uplands to their work and between villages, or ambled up and down on the backs of Galician horses, as did José of Parada and Novoneyra himself, as a young man. To go slowly in a terrain gives rise to a need for many names, and a rich lexicon of the land emerges. Going faster (by cart, by car, by plane), humans see less, need less, have less to say. To walk less is in fact to lose the ability to speak. Novoneyra uses, preserves, savours Courelian speech. As a result, reading him, we can walk again in the land. As Novoneyra said in 1992: "The function of poetry is to create a new sensibility." His vocabulary does this with us, in us.

with thanks to the words and images in Galician (for even young Galicians need explanations of Courelian Galician) at www.slideshare.ent/monadela/novoneyra-o-courel-a-paisaxe

In Erín Moure's *Little Theatres*, in its original Galician and its EM translation, there is a poem that tells of a solitude so deep that the poet adopts a raindrop. Even though she'd not yet read Novoneyra when she wrote it in 2002, she'd spent weeks in rural Galicia and

A gramática do can

Teño un pequeniño can de auga
É soamente unha cavilla pequena
o meu can de auga

¿Velo
tan esgotado
atrás da leira
có fociño acochado na herba dobrada?

É o meu can de auga.
Cada folla de herba mólla unha bufanda na súa pasaxe.

Mesma a herba hoxe está correndo.
Mesma a herba hoxe toca o can de auga.

was caught up in the *conxuro* of rain and of the land. Somehow this poem has touched folks in the intervening years; more than once Moure has been recognized, across a metro car or in the street, with the sudden outcry: *Dog of water! dog of water!*

The grammar of the dog

I have a little dog of water
It is just a little peg
my dog of water

Do you see it
so worn down
across the little field
nosing low in the bended grasses?

It is my dog of water.
Each leaf of grass dips a scarf into its passing.

Even the grass today is running.
Even the grass today touches the dog of water.

First published in *Little Theatres*, Toronto: House of Anansi, 2005, 46-47.

ACKNOWLEDGMENTS

Thanks to Uxío Novoneyra Rei, Branca Novoneyra Rei, and Elba Rei for the generous permission of the Fundación Uxío Novoneyra to permit this special edition in English of some poems from *Os Eidos* (The Uplands), along with a few from *Elexías* (Elegies) and *Do Courel a Compostela* (From The Courel to Compostela). Thanks to Antón Lopo for letting me reprint my translation of his essay on Novoneyra, and a bit of text from his biography of the poet, *A Distancia do Lobo* (Distance of the Wolf). Thanks too to House of Anansi Press for permission to reproduce my own poem. And to Chan da Pólvora for permission to select from the notes of Emilio Araúxo. And to Chus Pato, for support in all things.

As an outdoor kid, one who grew up in the shadow of the Canadian Rockies and who has always lived with respiratory illness, I find a dwelling place in the language and poems of Uxío Novoneyra. As child of a rural mother whose gaze lay with the Land, even after she went blind, I read his poems with my fingers and with my skin and ears, and feel the high wind in them. The book is wide and square to let the reader hold space in their hands, to let the reader receive not just the poems but the silences and vocables and snows and winds of the mountain lands and high-sloped fields—cultivated since late Neolithic times—in which they were written. Just as I first received them in Galician. With thanks, with awe. I print only some of the originals, which is unusual, I know. I wished of course that readers get a sense of the Galician, and of what is wrought in the translations. But I also wanted the musics—the lexical movement and splendour—of each poem to refract off that of neighboring poems, as it does in Galician, without pointing the reader overly toward comparison. There is an *experience of the book* that I wanted to convey. A dwelling. Words emerging from high mists, like tracks of wolves still present, yet already gone.

Thanks to *Arkansas International* and *Dispatches from the Poetry Wars* in the USA, and *above/ground press* in Canada, where some of these translations first appeared.

Novoneyra is a caesura where the world suspends its pulsing din and the world trembles and glows like a star. With him, we are a people who stride onward, and our striving is never in vain.

–Chus Pato, author of *Secession*

Uxío Novoneyra was one of the greatest Galician poets of the 20th century. He was devoted to his region, the mountainous Courel, to its variant of Galician and to its names and ways, as well as to Galician culture and language as a whole. He defended the expression of minority cultures everywhere and their–and our–freedom from imperialism, war, and capital's expansionist oppression. He was an eco-poet before the concept existed. Maybe he even invented it. He wrote and rewrote one great book all his life, *Os Eidos* [*The Uplands*], from which most of these poems are drawn.

VELIZ BOOKS

ISBN 9781949776041

51800 >

9 781949 776041